The Life Cycle of Plants

by Howard Warren

Table of Contents

Introduction 2
Chapter 1 The Seed 4
Chapter 2 Plant Reproduction 10
Chapter 3 How Seeds Are Spread 18
Conclusion 22
Glossary 23
Index 24

Introduction

The life cycle of a plant begins with a seed. It ends when the grown plant produces new seeds. In between, the plant grows, develops, and matures. It flowers and spreads its seeds to other areas. More plants grow and others die. The cycle goes on and on.

You probably know plants are living things. Plants needs air, water, light, and in most cases, a place to bury their roots in order to grow. But did you know that the plant dies if any of these ingredients are missing?

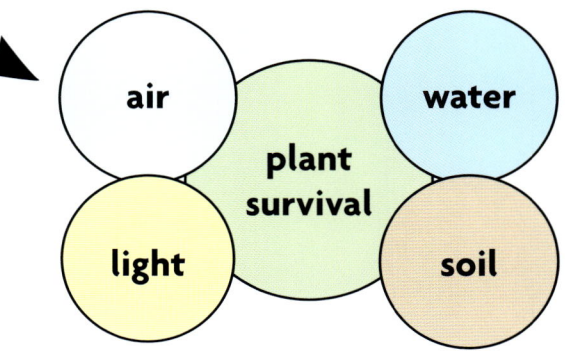

▲ Plants need air, water, light, and good soil to survive.

▲ Plants were on Earth long before the dinosaurs.

In this book, you will learn how plants grow from seed to flowering plant. You will read about a plant's life cycle. Plants have been around for a long time. They were on Earth before humans. Plants are important to everyone. They are food for animals and humans. We could not live without plants. Read on to learn more about amazing plants!

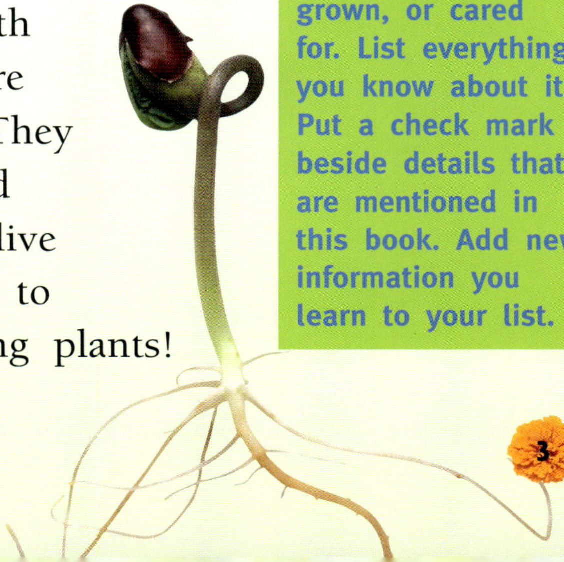

✓ POINT

Make Connections

Think of a plant you have seen, grown, or cared for. List everything you know about it. Put a check mark beside details that are mentioned in this book. Add new information you learn to your list.

CHAPTER 1

The Seed

Most plants begin life as a seed. Seeds come in many different sizes and shapes. A mustard seed is as small as a grain of sand. A coconut seed is as large as a human head. Seed shapes are amazingly varied, too. Some seeds, like the round pea, have very simple shapes. Others look as strange as an insect.

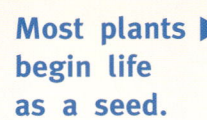
▶ Most plants begin life as a seed.

▲ Seeds come in many sizes, shapes, and colors.

Seeds have important roles in many cultures around the world. They can be food, medicines, fuel, art, and even musical instruments. Doctors have used plants as medicine for thousands of years. In South Africa, large seeds are strung together and worn as ankle bracelets. Some Native American tribes put seeds inside empty turtle shells to make rattles.

Seeds also play an important role in art. They are used to make beautiful murals, masks, and jewelry.

As important as seeds are to human beings, the most important job a seed has is to grow into a new plant.

The aloe plant has ▶ been used as medicine for hundreds of years.

CHAPTER 1

The Biology of a Seed

One seed contains everything needed to make a new plant. The seed has three important parts it needs to make a new plant. The three parts are the seed coat, the **cotyledon** (kah-tuh-LEE-dun) and the **embryo** (EM-bree-oh), or baby plant.

The seed coat is a protective skin that covers the entire seed. It absorbs water and keeps the seed moist. The seed coat allows water to pass through to reach the cotyledon. The cotyledon is the plant's early food source. It looks like tiny leaves.

As it absorbs water, the seed swells. If the air is warm enough, the seed will **germinate** (JUHR-mih-nayt), or begin to grow into a plant. The first part of plant development occurs in the dark. The seed does not need light in order to germinate.

When a seed germinates, the embryo inside it begins to grow. The embryo is the part that will will develop into the mature plant.

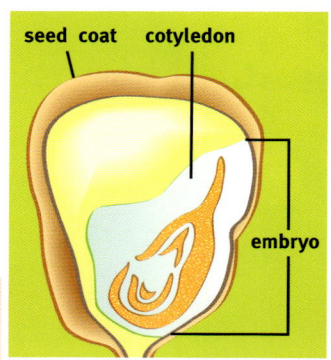

◀ This cross-section shows a seed's seed coat, cotyledon, and embryo.

THE SEED

HANDS-ON EXPERIMENT

You can perform an experiment that proves a seed does not need light to germinate.

Materials:
- Self-sealing plastic bag
- A lima bean seed or a kidney bean seed
- A paper towel
- A glass of water

Things to do:
1. Wet the paper towel and wring it out so it is moist.
2. Lay the damp towel flat on your desk or table.
3. Put the seed in the middle of the towel.
4. Fold the towel neatly around the seed.
5. Put the towel containing the seed in the plastic bag and seal the bag.
6. Place the bag in a safe, dark spot. Protect the seed from light.
7. Check your seed every day to see any changes that occur.
8. Draw your seed every time you check its progress and write down the date.

Make your own chart to record what you see.

DAY 1	DAY 2	DAY 3	DAY 4	DAY 5
DAY 6	DAY 7	DAY 8	DAY 9	DAY 10

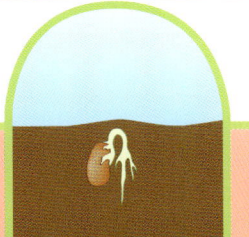

CHAPTER 1

The Plant Begins to Grow

The root is the first part of the embryo to peek out from between the two halves of the seed. It works its way down into the soil. The root searches for moisture in the soil. The roots of the plant absorb water from the soil. The water travels from the roots to all parts of the plant through a system of tiny tubes.

The **stem** appears next. It grows upward in search of light. The stem carries the cotyledon with it. These tiny seed leaves dry up and drop off the plant when the true leaves grow. You can see the true leaves before they begin to grow if you split a seed in half.

The stem grows upward, searching for light.

The Sprout Forms the True Plant

As the plant produces leaves, it is able to make more food. The plant grows and begins to mature. You will know this is happening when the plant makes a bud. A bud is the beginning of a flower. At this point, the plant is called a **sprout**.

▲ The sprout is a growing plant.

Besides air, water, and soil, a growing plant needs light. Sunlight helps the plant make its own food. This process is called **photosynthesis** (foh-toh-SIN-thuh-sus). Without light, photosynthesis cannot happen. The plant cannot make the food it needs to survive.

▲ Photosynthesis is how a plant makes its food.

Here is how photosynthesis works. The leaves of the plant have tiny holes that take in the gas **carbon dioxide** (KAR-bun dy-AHK-side) from the air. Photosynthesis happens when the carbon dioxide, water, and light combine. This causes the plant to produce the food the plant needs to grow.

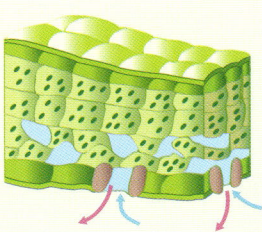

▲ Tiny holes let plants take in carbon dioxide.

CHAPTER 2

Plant Reproduction

Once a plant is fully grown, it flowers. Then the flower can **reproduce** (REE-pruh-doos), or make new plants. Plants have both male and female parts. The male part is called the **stamen** (STAY-mehn). The stamen produces the male reproductive cells. The female part is called the **pistil** (PIH-stuhl).

The female cells are in the egg sac, or ovary (OH-vah-ree), at the base of the stigma. The male reproductive cells travel through the style to the egg sac. When a male reproductive cell touches a female reproductive cell, the female cell becomes **fertilized** (FUHR-tih-lyzd) and begins to grow.

▶ Plants have both male and female reproductive parts.

Pollen in the Air

How do flowers grow? A mature male reproductive cell must combine with a mature female reproductive cell.

In order for the cells to meet, **pollen** containing the male reproductive cells of one flower has to get to the female reproductive cells of another flower from the same kind of plant. This process is called **pollination** (PAH-lih-nay-shuhn). Tiny grains that look like dust are in pollen.

A flower cannot walk over to another flower to deliver pollen. The plant depends on the wind, insects, animals, and humans to do the job.

▲ These are a flower's stamen.

▲ This is a flower's stigma.

It's a Fact

The pollen grain of each type of flower is unique. Because of this, it is impossible for the pollen of a rose to fertilize a daisy or any other kind of flower.

Plant Fertilization

When a breeze passes over a flower, many grains of pollen are carried along in the air. Most pollen grains never make it to another flower. Each flower produces so many pollen grains, though, that enough find their way to another plant. The stigma acts as a sticky landing zone on the flower. Some pollen grains are carried to the stigma by a breeze. Others are carried by insects. Insects fly from flower to flower.

When the pollen grains land on the sticky stigma, a tube opens inside the stigma. The male reproductive cells go down the tube and into the egg sac. When the male reproductive cells reach the egg sac, they fertilize the eggs.

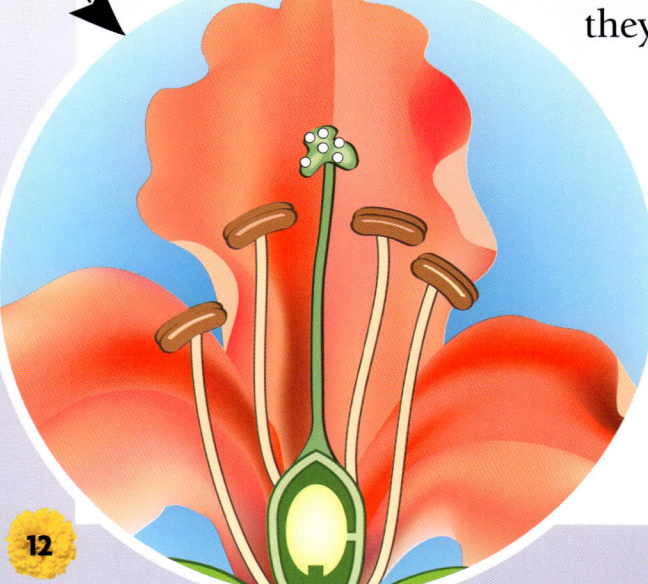

◀ Pollen attaches to the stigma of a flower.

PLANT REPRODUCTION

Next, the fertilized egg begins to develop into a seed. When this happens, the petals of the flower begin to fall off. The egg sac swells and becomes the seeds of the plant. When the seeds of the plant mature, they fall from the plant. When the seeds fall to the ground, the plant's life cycle is complete.

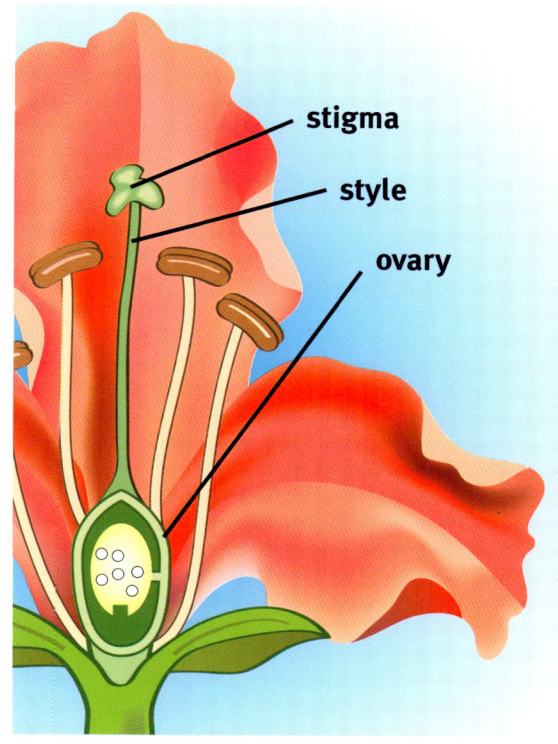

▲ When a plant is fertilized, it can start to make a new plant.

IT'S A FACT

Millions of people are allergic to pollen. People who suffer from pollen allergies can be allergic to only one type of pollen or they can be allergic to many. During the spring and summer, weather reports tell how much tree and grass pollen is present in the air.

13

CHAPTER 2

Insects and Flowers

Do you know that plants advertise? When they are ready to reproduce, plants send signals to insects and birds. Many insects and birds are attracted to the beautiful colors of the flowers. Others respond to the plant's scent, or smell.

Bees are drawn to plants by sweet smells. They follow the scents to the flowers. Flowers reward insects with a sweet treat called **nectar** (NEHK-tuhr). Bees use nectar to make honey.

As bees collect nectar from a flower, they brush against the flower's pollen. They carry pollen grains to the next flower they visit. They brush the pollen from the last flower onto the sticky stigma of the new flower.

It's a Fact

Some flowers that look plain to the human eye have beautiful infrared patterns. Some insects can see infrared, and these patterns lead them right to the pollen.

PLANT REPRODUCTION

False Advertising

Not all flowers have a pleasant, sweet smell. Some flowers have no smell at all. Other flowers don't smell good. Some flowers smell like dead animals or animal waste. Flies are attracted to those smells. They believe they will be feasting on a dead animal or animal droppings.

When the insect lands on one of these flowers, the insect brushes against the pollen as it searches for food. When it finds no nectar or food, the insect flies away, taking pollen grains with it. These pollen grains get deposited on the sticky stigma of the next flower the insect lands on.

▲ Insects carry pollen from one flower to the next.

Math Matters

Scientists believe a honeybee pollinates a flower once every fifteen minutes. That means in an eight-hour day, a single honeybee would reach thirty-two flowers. Sounds like a lot of work!

CHAPTER 2

Some flowers are very tricky. The reproductive parts of many orchids look like female insects. The male insect is lured to the orchid. When he grabs on to what he thinks is a female insect, he is swung into the pollen. When he realizes that this was just a case of mistaken identity, he flies off.

▲ orchid

The insect makes the same mistake again. He spots another orchid that looks like a female insect. He lands in the flower. The male insect picks up more pollen, but he also deposits some pollen from the previous plant. An insect can cover a wide area in a day. As the pollen dries, it falls as the insect flies. This way, the pollen gets spread wherever the insect flies.

They Made a Difference

Carl Linnaeus (1707–1778) is often referred to as the "father of modern botany." Botany is the study of plants. His work in classifying different types of plants is still in use today.

PLANT REPRODUCTION

▲ Tomatoes and cucumbers are really fruits.

Don't Eat the Fruit!

When we think of fruit, we think of apples, oranges, peaches, and plums. Humans can eat many types of fruit produced by plants, but not all. Some fruits are poisonous to humans, like the fruit of poison ivy and the chokecherry.

Some things we call vegetables are actually fruit. Green peppers, tomatoes, and cucumbers are often called vegetables. In fact, these are really fruits. They all contain seeds. Any "vegetable" that contains seeds is a fruit!

How Seeds Are Spread

Seeds need to find a place to grow. The shape of a seed gives clues as to how it does this. Dandelion and milkweed seeds are attached to feathery stalks. Sometimes people pick dandelions and blow the seeds off their stem. This is how their seeds travel.

▲ People sometimes spread dandelion seeds.

Many seeds have tiny hooks. These seeds are like hitchhikers. They hitch a ride to a new place where they will land and grow. Wild animals often transport these seeds. The seeds get caught in the animals' fur. People transport seeds, too. Seeds can get stuck on shoelaces, socks, or sweaters. When you brush the seeds off your clothes, they find new places to grow.

Plants that grow near the shoreline may have their seeds drift in the water until they get washed up on land. The coconut seed can drift for long distances before it washes up on shore.

Fruits with seeds provide food for many animals. Bears eat blueberries. Deer eat apples. Birds eat blackberries. Each of those animals spread seeds through the forest. How? The animals digest the fruit, but they cannot digest the seeds. This is because the seed coat protects the seed. As the animal travels through the forest, the seeds are left behind in the animal's waste. Animal waste is good fertilizer and helps the seeds grow.

Everyday Science

One plant whose seeds are "hitchhikers" is the cocklebur.

▲ Some seeds drift in the water until they find a spot to germinate.

CHAPTER 3

▼ Thorns are no defense against insects.

The Interrupted Cycle

Plants are under constant attack by animals. Animals need plants to survive. When animal populations become too large, plant life is destroyed. In the northeastern United States, there are so many deer that they have eaten many of the plants in the forest.

Many plants have thorns to keep animals from munching their leaves. But thorns are no defense against insects. A single swarm of insects can destroy entire crops. The tiny leaf miner insect digs tunnels through leaves. Japanese beetles feast on the leaves of roses.

HOW SEEDS ARE SPREAD

Weather

Severe weather and storms can damage or kill plants. Hail acts like an artillery attack in the summer. Ice storms freeze the tender shoots of plants in the early spring. Spring floods drown plants and rot seeds. Droughts also cause damage and death to plants. Some plants survive the natural disasters. Many do not. They are unable to complete their life cycles.

The most dangerous animals to Earth's plant population are humans. When a city gets crowded, people build outside the city. Trees and plants are bulldozed to make way for highways and more houses. The development can cause an increase in pollution. Pollution affects the health of the plant world. Scientists are working hard to make sure we keep plants healthy.

▲ Locusts can destroy a field of crops in a very short time.

✓ POINT

Read More About It

Algae! Snake beans! The Venus Fly Trap! Ask your teacher or librarian to help you find information on these and other unusual plants in books or on the Internet.

Conclusion

Plants are very important to all living creatures on Earth. Animals, insects, and humans need plants for food. They all must work together.

You can help. Start a life cycle for a plant. All you need to do is plant a seed and watch it grow!

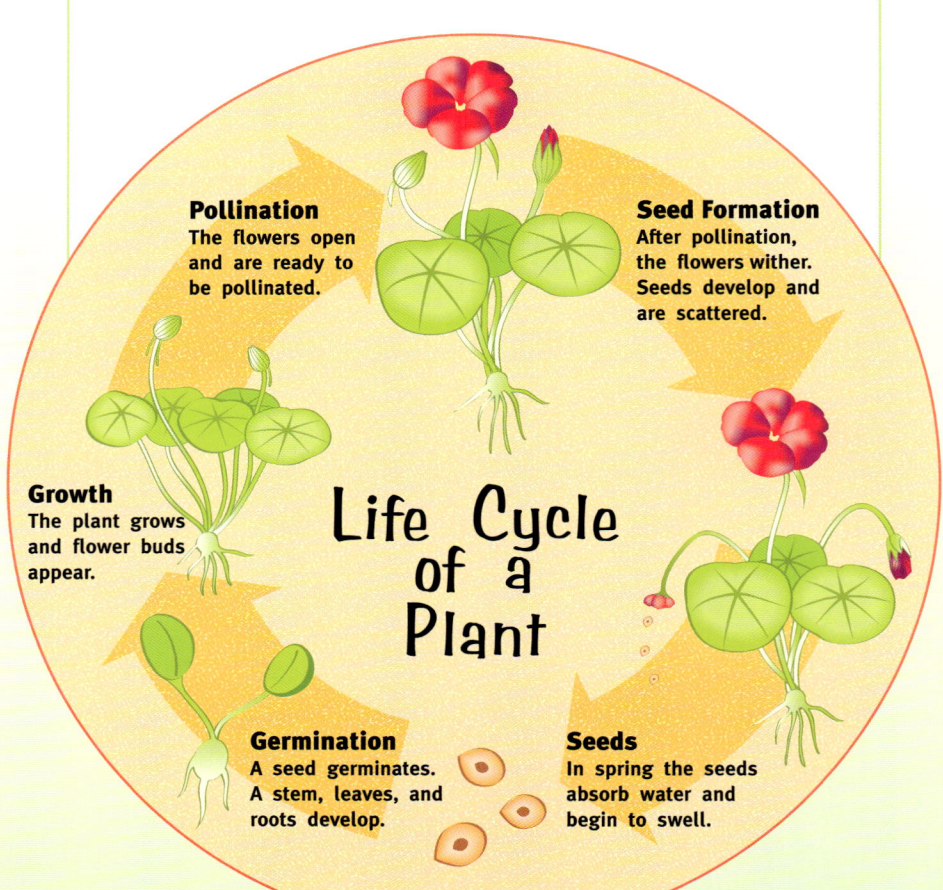

Life Cycle of a Plant

Pollination
The flowers open and are ready to be pollinated.

Seed Formation
After pollination, the flowers wither. Seeds develop and are scattered.

Growth
The plant grows and flower buds appear.

Germination
A seed germinates. A stem, leaves, and roots develop.

Seeds
In spring the seeds absorb water and begin to swell.

Glossary

carbon dioxide (KAR-bun dy-AHK-side) a gas that plants use to make food (page 9)

cotyledon (kah-tuh-LEE-dun) the first food source for a germinated seed (page 6)

embryo (EM-bree-oh) an early stage of plant development (page 6)

fertilize (FUHR-tih-lyz) to unite male and female reproductive cells in plants (page 10)

germinate (JUHR-mih-nayt) to sprout, as from a seed (page 6)

nectar (NEHK-tuhr) liquid found in flowers and used by bees to make honey (page 14)

photosynthesis (foh-toh-SIN-thuh-sus) the process plants use to make food from water, carbon dioxide, and light (page 9)

pistil (PIH-stuhl) the female reproductive part of a flower (page 10)

pollen (PAH-lihn) the part of a flower that carries male reproductive cells (page 11)

pollination (PAH-lih-nay-shuhn) the transfer of pollen from one plant to another (page 11)

reproduce (REE-pruh-doos) to make a new plant (page 10)

sprout (SPROWT) new plant growth from a seed (page 9)

stamen (STAY-mehn) the male reproductive part of a flower (page 10)

stem (STEHM) the hollow part of plant that carries water and nutrients to the leaves (page 8)

Index

carbon dioxide, 9

cotyledon, 6, 8

embryo, 6, 8

fertilize, 10, 12–13

germinate, 6

nectar, 14–15

ovary, 10

photosynthesis, 9

pistil, 11

pollen, 11–12, 14–16

pollination, 11

reproduce, 10, 14

root, 8

seed, 2–7, 13, 17–19, 21–22

sprout, 9

stamen, 10

stem, 8

stigma, 10, 12, 14–16